CLEP

Sociology
2012

Condensed Summary and Test Prep Guide

By David C. Haus and Michael D. Haus

ISBN#: 978-1611046007

Published by:

Feather Trail Press, LLC
P. O. Box 7
Cedar Lake, Michigan 48812

Table of Contents

Famous People

Arlie Hochschild (1940—):
- proposed that the American family was stuck in a stalled gender revolution in his book "Second Shift"

Auguste Comte (1798-1857):
- French philosopher
- the first to develop the concept of "sociology"
- founder of sociology and the doctrine of positivism
  - developed positivism in an attempt to remedy the malaise caused by the French Revolution
  - proposed that data derived from sensory experience, together with logical and mathematical treatments of such data, are the exclusive source of all authoritative knowledge
- helped lay the foundation for the humanist movement
- defined the "Law of Three Stages"
  - how societies progress through three stages—theological, metaphysical, and positivist or scientific

C. Wright Mills:
- developed the concepts of Power Elite Political Structure and Sociological Imagination
  - Power Elite Political Structure—proposes that an intricate set of overlapping small but dominant groups (top leaders in the business, government, and military) dominate the political structure and decisions in the United States
  - Sociological Imagination— refers to the ability to see the relationship between individual experiences and the larger society

Charles Horton Cooley (1864-1929):
- founding member and 8th president of the American Sociological Association
- best known for developing the concept of the "Looking Glass Self"
    - a person's self grows out of society's interpersonal interactions and the perceptions of others
    - self-concept is reevaluated every time the person enters a new social situation
    - divided into three stages:
        1. We imagine how we must appear to others
        2. We imagine the judgment of that appearance
        3. We develop our self through the judgments of others
    - the end result is that self-concept is based on the judgments of others, who become our "looking glass" or mirror
        - e.g. people see themselves as they perceive others seeing them
- defined "Primary" and "Secondary" groups
    - primary group members interact intimately and warmly over a long period of time (e.g. families, friends, neighbors, and church members)
    - secondary group members interact much less, develop few emotional ties, and may be anonymous or only part of the group for a short duration (e.g. a stockbroker and his clients)

Edwin Sullivan (1883-1950):
- American sociologist of the Symbolic Interactionist school of thought
- one of the most influential criminologists of the 20th century
- best known for defining white-collar crime and differential association
    - white collar crime is non-violent crime committed by a person of respectability and high social status in the course of his occupation
    - differential association proposed that individuals learn the values, attitudes, techniques and motives for criminal behavior through interaction with others

Émile Durkheim (1858-1917):
- Frenchman and first sociologist to systematically apply scientific methods to sociology
  - relied extensively on statistics in his sociological research
  - believed that sociologists should consider observable, or objective evidence only
- taught that humans were different from other animals
  - animals are satisfied once their biological needs are met
  - humans desire a higher sense of purpose to reach fulfillment
- proposed that society limits the insatiable desires of humans and gives meaning to their lives
  - society is the answer to the human need for higher fulfillment, and therefore a source of moral and mental life
- famous for his definition of four types of suicide
  - egoistic (results from too little social integration)
  - altruistic (results from too much social integration, e.g. voluntary self-sacrifice in the military)
  - anomic (results from not having the means to fulfill needs)
  - fatalistic (occurs in those with overregulated, unrewarding lives—i.e. slaves
- proposed that a limited amount of crime is necessary and beneficial for society
- defined the "Functionalist Perspective," which proposes that:
    - each part of society contributes to its overall stability
    - everything, whether apparently good or bad, serves some kind of function
    - the various aspects of society are interdependent
    - practicality, purpose, and utility are very important
    - functions are necessary in the establishment of group boundaries, as they mark the extremities of acceptable behavior
- adopted a functional approach to his study of religion
  - proposed that religion acts as a source of solidarity and identification for the individuals within a society by affirming their common beliefs and values on a regular basis
  - believed that every day, secular, or worldly aspects of life are profane
    - there should be a division between the sacred and the profane

- sacred objects, beliefs, and rituals should be set apart as supernatural & special
  - wrote "The Elementary Forms of Religious Life"
    - a work based on his study of Australian aborigines
  - stated that religion is more than a set of beliefs, since its regular rituals and ceremonies keep a sense of group solidarity among the members
- known for his functionalist view of deviance
  - his anomie theory proposed that the cause of deviance is a state of normlessness resulting from rapid social change
    - anomie is the confusion that arises when social norms conflict or don't exist
    - anomie refers to a condition of relative normlessness
      - social regulations break down
      - the controlling influence of society on individual propensities is no longer as effective
      - individuals are left to their own devices
      - change could result in anomie either in the whole society or some parts of it
- defined "organic solidarity" as:
  - the "glue" that holds complex societies together
  - social cohesion found in industrial societies, where people perform very specialized tasks and feel united by their mutual dependence

Erik Erikson (1902-1994):
- studied under Sigmund Freud for numerous years
- expanded upon Freud's psychoanalytic ideas and, like Freud, defined the stages of human development
- suggested that development proceeds in a healthy fashion as developmental crises are confronted and resolved
- believed the primary task of adolescence is to develop an identity
- developed unique views on human development and the psychosocial stages, which differ from Freud's in three key areas, including:
  - Erikson placed substantially less importance on the individual's sexual drive as a factor in normal development
  - Erikson focused on the psychosocial while Freud focused on the psychosexual

- o Erikson placed a much greater emphasis on social and cultural forces (and less on the importance of maturation) than Freud
- o Erikson did not believe that a failure at any stage of development would cause irreversible harm to the individual
- o Erikson defined stages of human development that cover the entire lifespan, while Freud's theory ends with adolescence

Ernest Burgess (1886-1966):
- wrote "Science of Sociology" in collaboration with Robert Ezra Park in 1921
  - o one of the most influential sociology books ever written
- developed the Concentric Zone Model for cities, which proposed that due to land values, cities usually develop into five zones:
  - o Zone 1: Central Business District
  - o Zone 2: Transitional District (mixes industrial with deteriorating housing)
  - o Zone 3: Working class / residential / tenemants
  - o Zone 4: Higher class residential zones
  - o Zone 5: Commuter / suburban zones

Erving Goffman (1922-1982):
- developed the concept of symbolic interaction in the form of dramaturgical analysis
- proposed that social interaction resembled a drama or play
  - o people play roles much as actors do
  - o people attempt to control the reactions of others by presenting a certain image of themselves
- defined symbolic interaction as the patterns of communication, interpretation and adjustment between individuals

George Herbert Mead (1863-1931):
- American philosopher who studied the nature of self
- one of the founders of social psychology and the American sociological tradition in general
- proposed that the self develops through three stages:
  1. preparatory stage (when children imitate others)
  2. play stage (when children take on the roles of specific people)
  3. game stage (when children become aware of the expectations of others

- suggested that process of acting involves the interaction of two basic aspects of the self, the I and the Me
- famous as a pragmatist
  - pragmatism is the philosophical attitude that the value of an idea lies in its practical consequences
- developed the theory of Symbolic Interactive Perspective
  - society is the sum of face-to-face interactions of individuals and groups
  - focuses on a microlevel of analysis

Gustave Le Bon (1841-1931):
- French sociologist
- famous for developing theories about crowd psychology (e.g. the Contagion Theory)
  - explained unconventional collective behavior by stating that:
    - being in a crowd frees individual members from feelings of responsibility or social restraint
    - because crowd members feel anonymous, they are willing to "follow the crowd" even in harmful, illegal, or unconventional behavior

Herbert Gans (1927—):
- influential American sociologist
- famous as a critic of urban renewal and for his book "Urban Villagers"

Herbert Spencer (1820-1903):
- English philosopher who developed an all-embracing conception of evolution as the progressive development of the physical world, biological organisms, the human mind, and human culture and societies
- enthusiastic proponent of evolution who was said to have written about evolution before Darwin did
- promoted the sociological concept of functionalism
  - laid the foundation for functionalism in his writings
    - each part of society contributes to its overall stability
    - everything, good or bad, serves some kind of function

Jacob L. Moreno:
- developed the technique of sociometry
  - a quantitive method for measuring social relationships
  - helps researchers to determine who is interacting with whom and find the direction of interaction in a small group

Jean Piaget (1896-1980):
- noted Swiss developmental psychologist and psychological researcher
- initially trained as a biologist and naturalist
- became a psychologist later in his career
- best known for his studies in ethology and groundbreaking work in developmental psychology
- followed the Cognitive Theory of Development
- theorized that cognitive development proceeds in four sequentially, genetically determined stages which may be achieved at different speeds by different children, and developed the Four Stages of Cognitive Development:
  1. Sensorimotor Stage
     - extends from birth to the acquisition of language
     - includes causality (children begin to learn that some events have knowable causes and some behaviors cause predictable reactions)
       - children discover by sensing and by doing
       - object permanence develops by the end of this stage
  2. Preoperational Stage
     - development stage where the child's thinking is egocentric or self-centered
       - their view is the "only possible one"
       - they are incapable of seeing things from another point of view
       - they start to understand that they are an independent and separate person
       - they are not selfish—just can't see things from another person's point of view
  3. Concrete Operational Stage
     - occurs between 7 and 11 years of age
     - characterized by the appropriate use of logic

- ability to sort objects, recognize relationships, name and identify items, advanced problem solving, and the ability to see things from another's perspective (elimination of egocentrism)
  - able to solve problems that apply to actual (concrete) objects or events
  - not yet ready to handle abstract concepts or hypothetical tasks
  4. Formal Operational Stage
    - includes logical use of symbols related to abstract concepts, hypothetical and deductive reasoning, and the ability to operate by individually governed moral standards
    - takes place between adolescence and adulthood

Karl Marx (1818-1883):
- taught that the economy is the base upon which the superstructure of all other social institutions is erected
- proposed that all societies are marked by "Class Conflict," where the poor are exploited by the rich and powerful
- believed that social classes were invariably unequal and would determine property ownership
- stated that capitalist society consists of two classes, the Proletariat (laborers) and the Bourgeoisie (those with power and wealth), who are in constant conflict:
  - the Bourgeoise, who own property and the means of production, invariably exploit the Proletariats
  - property ownership is determined by class
  - someday the Proletariats would overthrow the Bourgeoisie, and a class-free society would be established
- defined "False Consciousness" as a social condition in which the working class possess a distorted perception of the reality of class and its consequences
  - the workers fail to recognize themselves as a class
  - the workers are blind to the adversarial relationship that naturally exists between themselves and the capitalists
- called religion "the opium of the masses"

- o theorized that religion lulls people into believing their current state of exploitation is acceptable, just as opiates provide a false sense of well-being

Kingsley Davis (1908-1997):
- American sociologist noted, with Wilbert E. Moore, for an explanation and justification for social stratification based the concept of "functional necessity."
- coined the terms "population explosion" and "zero population growth"

Lewis Killian (1919-2010):
- together with Ralph Turner proposed the Emergent-Norm Theory:
    - theorizes that new norms or expected behaviors, which are created by a few individuals, are soon adopted by the whole crowd (e.g. doing the "wave" at a sporting event)

Margaret Mead (1901-1978):
- American cultural anthropologist
- frequently a featured writer and speaker in the mass media in the 1960s and 1970s
- famous for her Theory of Male Aggressiveness
    - o higher levels of aggression exhibited by men resulted from an adaptive trait since in earlier times they needed to hunt and protect their family

Max Weber (1864-1920):
- coined the term "verstehen," which refers to empathy or putting oneself into another person's shoes
- developed the classic model of modern bureaucracy
    - o the formation of bureaucracies are inevitable due to the complex nature of modern life compounded by the growing demands placed on governments by their citizens
    - o believed promotion of bureaucrats should be gradual and based on merit rather than political connections
- defined "Charismatic Authority" as the ability to influence others through exemplary or extraordinary character attributes
- defined leadership "Legitimacy" as a state where people are led to believe that their leader has a legitimate right to command

- o authority is ultimately granted by those being governed—they must believe in the ruler or leader's legitimacy
- taught that "Social Power" is held by bureaucracies in modern society
- held that people of affluence have more opportunities in life than those who are poor
  - o differences in a person's opportunities for income, how other people assess that person's status, and the forming of parties to acquire social power, are all unavoidable sources of social stratification
- focused on the origins of man-made culture
  - o believed that due to class, status situation, and parties being a source of conflict and change, there was no foreseeable end to social stratification
- divided social stratification into two types:
  - o an open class system of stratification facilitates social mobility, with individual achievement and personal merit determining social rank
  - o a closed class system of stratification determines social status by birth right as opposed to personal accomplishment
- studied six of the world's largest religions to determine religion's impact on social change
  - o wrote the "Protestant Ethic and the Spirit of Capitalism"
  - o believed that Protestantism's "Work Ethic" played a large part in the development of capitalism in the West, whereas Eastern religions such as Hinduism were barriers to capitalism

Peter Berger (1929—)
- best known for proposing that social reality is a form of consciousness
- wrote about the relationship between society and the individual

Robert Ezra Park (1864-1944):
- American urban sociologist
- one of the most influential figures in American sociology
- wrote "Science of Sociology" in collaboration with Ernest Burgess in 1921
  - o one of the most influential sociology books ever written

Robert Merton (1910-2003):
- distinguished American sociologist who coined several well-known sociological terms including unintended consequences, reference group, role strain, role model, and self-fulfilling prophecy
- expanded on Durkheim's anomie theory (anomie is a state of normlessness)
  - proposed that there is often a gap between socially accepted goals and the means to accomplish them
    - e.g. many wish to gain wealth but do not have the means to obtain it
      - as a result they turn to deviance

Robert Michels (1876-1936):
- German sociologist who wrote on the political behavior of intellectual elites and contributed to elite theory
- best known for his book Political Parties, published in 1911, which contains a description of the "iron law of oligarchy"
- proposed that a small number of people actually make organizational decisions, even if the authority is supposed to belong to the members
  - despite the best of intentions, leaders grow continually more powerful and develop values which are at odds with the membership

Sigmund Freud: (1856-1939)
- Austrian neurologist and founder of psychoanalysis, which was based on his observations of many patients
  - psychoanalysis proposes that biological drives are the primary source of human activity
  - people are ruled through unconscious desires, and through socialization, learn to repress and channel these desires in socially acceptable ways
- studied personality development using techniques he designed to probe the hidden thoughts in the unconscious
- believed that too much or too little stimulation during any stage of human development could result in a fixation, leaving the person immature or incomplete in certain areas
  - argued that many adult personality problems could be traced to early fixations

14

- o if early experiences were free from upset or fixations, the individual was on the way to a healthy and normal adult life
- defined the erogenous zones as areas of the human body with heightened sensitivity
- defined five psychosexual stages of human development:
  1. Oral stage (birth to approximately 1 year old)
  2. Anal stage (roughly 1-3 years of age)
  3. Phallic stage (4-6 years of age)
  4. Latency stage (6 years to puberty)
  5. Genital stage (puberty to adulthood)
- saw the human personality as being divided into three parts:
  - Id (governed by the pleasure principle)
  - Ego (governed by the reality principle)
  - Superego (dominated by the morality principle)

Thomas Malthus (1766-1834):
- English scholar who popularized the theory of rent
- believed that population growth had a tendency to exceed food production
  - stated that the result of the food shortage would be wars, epidemics and finally famine

W. E. B. Du Bois (1868-1963):
- prominent African American sociologist
- coined the term Double-Consciousness, which referred to the identity of being both Black and American
- prolific author who wrote the book "Up from Slavery"

Wilbert E. Moore (1914-1987):
- American sociologist noted, with Kingsley Davis, for an explanation and justification for social stratification based the concept of "functional necessity."

William J. Goode (1917—2003)

- theorized that changing family patterns were more than a kneejerk reaction to industrialization
    - recognized that industrialization could support or help social change, although he didn't see it as the primary cause
- wrote the book "World Revolution and Family Patterns"
- noted a trend in industrialized societies toward nuclear family households, which he called "western conjugal family system"

Crime, Deviance, and Crowd Behavior

Collective Behavior:
- any group behavior, including:
  - short-lived, spontaneous public expressions of feeling
  - long-term public expressions aimed at achieving specific results
  - mass hysteria, panics, crazes, fads, fashions, and rumors
- is rarely random
- usually lacks institutional backing
- a collective response to changed culture or social circumstances

Contagion Theory:
- theory developed by Gustave Le Bon
- proposes that crowds exert a hypnotic influence over their members through collective suggestibility
  - in crowds, people tend to abandon their personal responsibilities and join in the emotions of the crowd about them
  - crowd members feel shielded by the anonymity of the crowd

Convergence Theory:
- proposes that a number of like-minded individuals coming together forms a collective action
  - individual motives resulted in the collective action, not some separate "collective mind of the crowd"
- contrasts with the Contagion Theory (mob mentality) developed by Gustave Le Bon

Crowd:
- a relatively large number of people in close proximity to each other
- sometimes characterized by suggestibility, emotional arousal, or feelings of anonymity
- have been divided into categories:

- Casual Crowd: loose collection of people gather around a specific event and interact briefly or not at all (e.g. shoppers in a mall or commuters on a city bus)
- Expressive Crowd: come together for the expression of strong emotion
- Acting Crowd: a crowd of people intensely focused on a specific purpose or goal (may erupt into violence)
- Conventional Crowd: gathers for a socially sanctioned purpose or event and are focused on that event (e.g. a concert or wedding)

Counterculture:
- a unique culture within a larger culture which does not conform to the larger culture's norms
- counterculture members often engage in unconventional behavior
  - e.g. political extremists

Deviance:
- any behavior which violates social norms
- can either be criminal or non-criminal
- varies depending on the norms for a society
  - e.g. alcoholism, public nudity, stealing, and cross-dressing are considered deviant in American society

Differential Association Theory:
- offers an explanation for how people learn deviance
- developed by Edwin Sullivan
- proposes that humans learn deviant behavior, like other behavior, from their interaction with others

Emergent-Norm Theory:
- theorizes that new norms or expected behaviors, which are created by a few individuals, are soon adopted by the whole crowd (e.g. doing the "wave" at a sporting event)
- proposed by Ralph Turner and Lewis Killian

General Deterrence:
- crime prevention through the instillation of fear in the general population through punishment of offenders

Genocide:
- the deliberate, systematic killing of an entire people or nation
  - e.g. the extermination of 6 million Jews by Nazi Germany in World War II

Group Conformity:
- matching personal attitudes, beliefs, and behaviors to group norms in response to peer pressure
  - conformists even comply with group goals that are in conflict with their own

Groupthink:
- occurs when the desire for group harmony in a decision-making group overrides a realistic appraisal of alternatives
- members of the group ignore reality in order to think similarly and conform to each other's views
- dissenting opinions are not tolerated, which prevents members with dissenting thoughts or alternate ideas from speaking out
- usually results in narrow-minded decisions

Individual Deterrence:
- where an individual offender is discouraged from further crimes through punishment

Mass behavior:
- behavior among people dispersed over a wide geographical area

Plea Bargain:
- legal negotiation in which the prosecution reduces a defendant's charge in exchange for a guilty plea or some other concession
- 90% of criminal convictions are obtained through plea bargaining rather than a trial

Rehabilitation:
- program for reforming criminal offenders into law-abiding citizens
- one of the goals of the penal system

Retribution:
- moral vengeance by which society inflicts suffering on an offender comparable to that caused by the offense
  - e.g. "the punishment should fit the crime"

Revolutionary Changes:
- movements seeking to bring about a total change in society
  - e.g. overthrow a government

Total Institution:
- place of work and residence where a great number of similarly situated people lead an enclosed, formally administered round of life
- place of forced re-socialization where the people confined are cut off from the rest of society
  - includes prisons, mental hospitals, and military bases

White Collar Crime:
- financially motivated, nonviolent crime committed for illegal monetary gain
  - e.g. forgery, fraud, embezzlement, counterfeiting
- white collar criminals are often respectable people with no previous criminal record

Economic Systems, Terms, and Stratification

Absolute Poverty:
- when a person doesn't have the means to afford the basic necessities

Agricultural Societies:
- agrarian societies where the chief occupation is agriculture
- depend on farming, but use techniques such as irrigation and draft animals to produce a large surplus
- more advanced than horticultural or pastoral societies, primarily due to the use of higher levels of technology
- produce large surpluses of food
- tend to be more permanent than horticultural or pastoral societies

American Dream:
- the belief that anyone may rise from poverty to wealth if they work hard enough

Barter System:
- form of distribution in which goods or services are exchanged directly for other goods or services considered to be of equivalent value
- the primary form of economic distribution before money became a medium of trade

Blue Collar Worker:
- manual laborer of the working class
- in contrast to White Collar (office) and Pink Collar (service) workers

Capitalism:
- private ownership of the means of production where personal profits are derived through market competition without government intervention

Collective Bargaining:
- work-related negotiations between employers and labor union leaders
- focused on pay rates, working conditions, fringe benefits, or similar issues

Contingent (Freelance) Work:
- part-time, temporary work that often involves sub-contracting
- allows employers to cut costs
- often found in jobs at schools, governments, and hospitals
- offers workers low pay and little job security

Deprofessionalization:
- the process by which some characteristics of a profession are eliminated
    - e.g. drug formulas, which Pharmacists used to prepare, are now formulated in factories

Economic Dependency Ratio:
- the number of people in the total population who are not in the total work force
    - the largest component of the dependency ratio is made up of those under 16
    - the fastest growing component consists of those over age 65

Economy:
- social institution that ensures the maintenance of society through the production, distribution, and consumption of goods and services

Free-Market System of Distribution:
- a market economy where:
    - decisions regarding investment, production and distribution are based on supply and demand
    - prices of goods and services are determined in a free price system
- money is used as a medium for trade

Glass Ceiling:
- artificial barrier in the work world which makes promotion beyond a certain level difficult for certain groups
- term first applied exclusively to women that later came to include minority men

Glass Elevator Theory (also known as Glass Escalator):
- rapid promotion of men over women, especially into management, in female-dominated fields such as nursing
  - some believe that men in such fields are promoted without having to make the usual struggle to advance
- based on the traditional stereotype that men are expected to be in chief roles with women in subordinate positions
- in fields where men are less common, they receive differential, favorable treatment that allows them to exert authority and control in the workplace
- opposite of the glass ceiling, where a seen but un-breachable barrier keeps minorities and women from rising to the upper rungs of the corporate ladder, regardless of qualifications or achievements
- theory was proposed by Christine Williams

Global Feminization of Poverty:
- income levels of men and women continue to widen
- globally, women are more impoverished than men

Goods:
- tangible products or materials intended to satisfy the wants or needs of a consumer
- buying and selling of goods is key to the economy

Horticultural Societies:
- grew their own food using a primitive level of technology
  - hand tools are used to farm
- were mobile societies that had to move as the land's resources were used up or water supplies dwindled

Hunting and Gathering Societies:
- nomadic groups that depend on hunting animals and gathering vegetation for food
- move constantly, relocating whenever food sources are depleted
- few such societies remain in the world (a few tribes in Africa and Malaysia would still be considered hunters and gatherers)

Income:
- economic gain derived from wages, salaries, income transfers, or property ownership

Industrial Society:
- a society driven by the use of technology to enable mass production, supporting a large population with a high capacity for division of labor
- came about in the 18th century, when the Industrial Revolution led to mechanization of production through complex, fuel-driven machines
- England was the first industrial society

Job Deskilling:
- where a job description is downgraded so that a reduction in proficiency is required to perform it
- often leads to a corresponding reduction in wages for that job
- usually occurs because of computers or other technological advances

Mechanical Solidarity:
- Durkheim's term for the unity that comes from being involved in similar occupations or activities
- refers to social cohesion in preindustrial societies, where there is a minimal division of labor and people feel united by shared values and common bonds

Meritocracy:
- form of social stratification in which all positions are awarded on the basis of merit
  - workers attain better jobs due to educational credentials instead of due to personal contacts

Net Worth:
- is usually higher for the married than the unmarried

Old Boy Network:
- social network that traditionally provided jobs to friends, family, and fellow alumni of the elite, mostly white, Protestant, male schools of the Northeast
  - women, people of color, and ethnic minorities were excluded from its benefits

Oligopoly:
- control of an entire industry by several large companies
  - e.g. the automobile manufacturing industry

Organic Solidarity:
- Durkheim's term for the interdependence that results from people needing others to fulfill their jobs
  - according to Durkheim, organic solidarity is the "glue" that holds complex societies together
- based on the interdependence brought about by the division of labor
  - social cohesion found in industrial societies, where people perform very specialized tasks and feel united by their mutual dependence

Pastoral Societies:
- a way of life based on the domestication of animals as a primary source of food
- still found in African societies where planting crops is not possible

Pay Gap:
- men usually make more than women
- the pay gap between women and men is about 77 cents an hour
- this is despite the fact that woman now earn more college bachelor's degrees than men

Peter Principle:
- a belief that in an organization where promotion is based on achievement, success, and merit, that organization's members will eventually be promoted beyond their level of ability

- competent managers tend to be given more authority and promoted until eventually they reach a position in which they are incompetent
- at that point, they don't receive further promotions; they're stuck in that position performing incompetently

Pink Collar Occupations:
- low-paying, non-manual, semi-skilled jobs held primarily by women

Pink Collar Workers:
- typically are service workers
- in contrast to White Collar (office) and Blue Collar (manual labor) workers

Postindustrial Societies:
- revolves around storing, manipulating, and selling information and services
- utilizes the latest technological advances
- the relative importance of services, information, and research grows even as the importance of manufacturing decreases

Primary Sector of the Economy:
- the part of the economy that produces raw materials and basic foods directly from the natural environment
- extracts or harvests products from the earth
  - includes activities such as hunting, gathering, farming, forestry, fishing, and mining

Pure Capitalism:
- economic system characterized by limited involvement of the government in the economy
  - productive resources are owned by individuals who can make use of those resources in any way they choose, subject to common productive legal restrictions
  - entrepreneurs pursue their own self-interest with few constraints
- contrasts with Welfare Capitalism, the system now in the United States
  - the government plays a major part in allocating resources

Quaternary Sector:
- consists of intellectual activities, including government, culture, libraries, scientific research, education, and information technology

Redlining:
- bank policy of refusing to make housing or business loans to people residing in low-income communities

Secondary Sector:
- the part of the economy that transforms raw materials into manufactured goods
  - includes mills and factories
  - raw materials become fuel, clothing, automobiles, etc.
  - includes all manufacturing, processing, and construction

Social Economic System:
- economic system where prices are set by the government and competition between producers is lacking

Society Types:
- there are six types of societies defined by sociologists, in order of complexity or technical advancement, beginning with the most primitive:
  - Hunting and gathering—primarily survive by hunting animals, fishing, and gathering plants
  - Pastoral societies—rely on cultivating fruits, vegetables, and plants
  - Agricultural societies—uses technological advances to cultivate crops
  - Feudal societies—based on ownership of land
  - Industrial societies—based on using machines, particularly fuel-driven ones, to produce goods
  - Postindustrial societies—based on information, knowledge, and the selling of services

Shared Monopoly:
- when four or fewer companies supply more than 50% of a given market
  - e.g. computer operating systems such as Microsoft's Windows

Tertiary Sector:
- that part of the economy which consists of service-oriented occupations
    - includes health, education, retail, transportation, distribution, entertainment, restaurants, and tourism

Underclass:
- small group of people for whom poverty persists year after year and across generations
    - they are poor, seldom employed, often on welfare, and generally trapped in a life of long-term deprivation

Upper Class:
- the social class composed of the wealthiest members of society, who also wield the greatest political power
    - usually consists of 1-2% of the population
    - in the United States the upper class is less than 1% of the population

Wallerstein's World Systems Theory:
- proposes that the world economic system must be understood as a single unit, not a collection of independent countries
- divides the world into three unequal economic categories:
    - periphery countries
        - poor countries that are exploited for cheap labor and raw materials
        - they sell raw materials and labors to core countries, then buy finished products from the core
        - primarily agricultural nations, found throughout Africa, Latin America, and Asia
    - semi-periphery countries
        - countries that are somewhat industrialized
        - exploit periphery countries and are themselves exploited by core countries
    - core countries
        - dominant capitalist industrialized countries
        - the most technologically advanced countries
        - exploit periphery and semi-periphery countries

Wealth:
- most often the result of inheritance rather than hard work
- in the United States, the wealthiest 20% of households earn 50% of the total income
- the wealthiest people receive large amounts of income, whereas the poorest receive comparatively very little

White Collar Worker:
- worker who typically performs a job in an office environment
- often sits at a computer or desk
- in contrast to Blue Collar (manual labor) and Pink Collar (service) workers

Working Class:
- those employed in lower-tier jobs
  - skilled, semi-skilled, and unskilled workers

Working Poor:
- those who live just above and just below the poverty line
- typically hold poorly paid unskilled or service sector jobs that offer little economic security
- live from paycheck to paycheck

Marriage, Family, Aging, and Gender Issues

Ageism:
- prejudice and discrimination against people on the basis of age
  - e.g. elder abuse

Attitude:
- generally positive or negative views of a person, place, thing, or event

Crude Death Rate:
- the number of deaths per 1,000 people in a population in a given year
  - The leading cause of death in:
    - the United States is heart disease
    - less developed countries is infectious disease

Divorce rates:
- between 40-60% of all new marriages end in divorce
  - divorce is more likely in situations with economic resources and low wages

Dyad:
- group of two people
- viewed as the most cohesive of all groups because of the potential for close and intense interaction
- larger groups tend to be less intimate
  - members in larger groups participate and cooperate less

Elder Abuse:
- refers to physical, psychological, financial, and/or medical abuse, exploitation or neglect of people aged 65 or older
- people over age 80 are the most common victims of elder abuse
- most victims are white women, and the perpetrators are usually their sons

- most cases of elder abuse go unreported because the victims are completely dependent upon their abusers for financial and material support
- almost unknown outside of the United States

Elderly:

- considered to be age 65 and older in most developed countries
- comprise the fastest growing age group in the United States, due to lower birth rates and higher life expectancy
- by the year 2030, the elderly (individuals over age 65) are expected to make up 22% of the U.S. population

Endogamy:

- marriage within a specific group (e.g. a Latino marrying a Latino)

Exogamy:

- marriage outside of a specific group

Extended Family:

- a nuclear family (father, mother, and their children) with the addition of other relatives such as a grandparent, cousin, aunt or uncle
- especially common in Asian societies where one dwelling may house three generations under the same roof

Family:

- people born into the same family of origin
  - people create their own families of procreation by having children or adopting them

Family of Orientation:

- group into which a person is born

Family of Procreation:

- group formed in adulthood by parents who have children

Fertility Rate:
- the number of children the average woman bears
- calculated by dividing the number of births in a year by the number of women aged 15 to 44, then multiplying that number by 1000

Gender Identity:
- personal preference for emotional sexual relationships with either members of the same sex, opposite sex, or both sexes
  - includes homosexuality, heterosexuality, and bisexuality

Gender Role:
- attitudes, behaviors, and activities that are socially defined as appropriate for each sex
- learned through the socialization process
  - the male gender role is more aggressive
  - the female role is more passive and nurturing

Gender Socialization:
- when parents treat their children differently depending on the sex of the child
  - female babies are more likely to be sung to and treated gently

Genitalia:
- the biological sex organs and primary sex characteristics

Illnesses:
- can be divided into two categories with regard to length:
  - chronic, or long-term, which last an entire lifetime
  - acute or short-term illness

Institution:
- a practice or relationship which is of importance in the life of a community or society (e.g. marriage or the family)
- an established organization dedicated to education, public service, or culture

Life Expectancy:
- the average lifetime of people born in a specific year
- longer in high-income nations, despite the fact that residents of such nations are more likely to eat high fat, junk food diets
- shorter in low-income nations due to high infant mortality rates

Matriarchy:
- family where the mother has the authority, or social system dominated by women

Matrilocality:
- when newlyweds live with the wife's family after their marriage

Medicalization:
- transformation of something into a matter to be treated by physicians
- practice of treating conditions such as drug addiction as medical conditions rather than individual behavioral choices

Middle Adulthood:
- ages between 40 and 65
- period of life when people's childrearing and career responsibilities often reach an end

Neolocality:
- when newlyweds live separately from their extended families after marriage

Nuclear Family:
- family unit containing only a mother, father, and their children
- dominant in the United States

Patriarchy:
- family where the majority of the authority is vested in the father

Patrilocality:
- when newlyweds live with the husband's family after marriage

Polygamy:
- where a marriage involves more than one spouse
  - e.g. when a man has more than one wife
- can be divided into two forms:
  - polyandry—where a woman has several husbands at once
  - polygyny—where a man has several wives at once

Second Shift:
- title of a book written by Arlie Hochschild
- proposed that the American family was stuck in a stalled gender revolution

Serial Monogamy:
- when a person marries more than one time during their lifetime, but is only married to one spouse at a time

Sexual activity:
- is more satisfying to people who are in sustained relationships such as marriage

Tracking:
- sorting of students into different educational programs on the basis of real or perceived abilities
  - affects student's academic achievement and their choice of careers

Triad:
- group of three people
  - not as cohesive and personal as a dyad (group of two)

Universal Health Care:
- health-care system where citizens receive medical services paid for by tax revenue

Voucher System:
- educational funding system that allows students and their families to spend money to purchase education at the school of their choice
  - controversial because they can result in radical shifts in funding from one school to another

Women in Sports:
- since the 1970's the number of American females involved in sports has dramatically increased
  - in 1971, only 1 in 27 high school girls played sports
  - by 1996, 1 in 3 high school girls played sports
  - in 1972, U.S. colleges averaged only two women's teams per campus
  - by 2002, that number increased to eight teams per campus

Women's Wages:
- women now earn about 75 percent of what men earn per hour worked
- the gap has been steadily closing

Zero Population Growth:
- where the number of births plus immigrants is equal to the number of deaths plus immigrants
  - e.g. people only have enough children to reproduce themselves

Power, Leadership, and Authority

Charismatic Authority:
- based on the ability to influence others through exemplary or extraordinary character attributes
- term coined by Max Weber
- gift shared by many politicians, including notorious ones such as Hitler or cult leaders

Expressive Leaders:
- are affiliation motivated (want to maintain warm, friendly relationships, and make sure that subordinates are satisfied)
- rely on a cooperative style of management instead the a directive style used by instrumental leaders (task-oriented leaders who are focused mainly on achieving their goals)

Instrumental Leaders:
- achievement motivated, task-oriented leaders who are focused on achieving their goals
- a directive management style
- often make good managers because they are efficient, but are not always well-liked by their subordinates
- in contrast to affiliation motivated leaders who rely on a cooperative style of management and emphasize maintaining warm, friendly relationships, and subordinate satisfaction

Iron Law of Oligarchy:
- proposes that rule by an elite, or "oligarchy", is inevitable as an "iron law" within any organization as part of the "tactical and technical necessities" of organization

Legitimacy:
- where people being led believe their leader has a legitimate right to command
- proposed by Max Weber, who believed that authority is ultimately granted by those being governed
- three ways to obtain legitimacy:
  - traditional
  - rational-legal
  - charismatic authority

Pluralist Model of Power:
- views power as dispersed among many competing interest groups
- because of the diversity of interests among the people, no one power can dominate society's decision-making process
- believed by David Riesman to exist in the United States

Power Elite Model of Political Structure:
- theory developed and term coined by C. Wright Mills and also the focus of his book "The Power Elite"
- proposes that an intricate set of overlapping small but dominant groups (top leaders in the business, government, and military) dominate the political structure and decisions in the United States
- the opposite would be the Pluralist Model, which maintains that power is dispersed throughout many competing interest groups

Traditional Authority:
- power legitimized through respect for long-established customs or cultural patterns
  - e.g. honoring or serving a king not because of the his qualifications, but because people in that culture have always honored and served the king

United States Supreme Court:
- vested with power to determine the constitutionality of United States laws
- judges on issues related to the separation of church and state

Racial, Ethnic, and Minority Issues

Amalgamation:
- the physical absorption of one group by another through intermarriage
- opposite of separation

Assimilation:
- when an immigrant group merges into the main culture by abandoning the culture of their homeland and gradually adopting the values of their new culture

Caucasian ethnicity:
- is predicted to severely decline by 2050

Chinese
- are the most numerous Asian Race in the United State (due to large scale immigration):

Diffusion:
- the spreading out of culture, culture traits, or a cultural pattern from a central point
- eventually occurs when two diverse cultures collide (e.g. through immigration or exploration)

Double-Consciousness:
- term coined by W.E.B. Du Bois to describe the identity of being both Black and American

Emigration:
- the act of permanently leaving one's country or region to settle in another

Ethnic Villagers:
- urban dwellers in tightly knit neighborhoods resembling small towns
  - often recent immigrants who feel most comfortable living among people of their own group
- one type of city resident, as defined by Herbert Gans' typology of urban dwellers

Ethnicity (Ethnic Differences):
- a group identified on the basis of their common language, national heritage, perspectives, distinctions, or cultural practices
  - a shared cultural heritage that defines a group of people
- based on culturally learned differences rather than race (which is based on physical characteristics)
- are learned and have nothing to do with genetics

Ethnocentrism:
- habit of judging all other cultures by comparison to one's own culture
- the individual sees his or her culture's way of doing things as "normal," or even superior
- a tendency that sociologists try to avoid
  - sociologists need to be objective when studying other cultures

Folkways:
- conventions, customs, or standards of behavior which members of a society or group expect conformity to
- are socially approved but not morally significant
- non-conforming individuals may seem peculiar or eccentric, but are not generally punished

Forceful relocation:
- during World War II nearly 120,000 Japanese-Americans were relocated from their homes into prison camps

Institutionalized Racism:
- racism which has been codified into society's institutions of custom, practice, and law
- discrimination which is built into the social structure
  - there is no identifiable perpetrator

Integration
- when ethnic minority groups remain distinctive, adapting and conforming to a limited number of majority values and behaviors
  - e.g. immigrating minority groups often maintain their own identity and religion while conforming to the majority legal system and system of commerce

Majority Group:
- a group that dominates within a particular society
- is advantaged with superior resources and rights

Physical Differences:
- are based on race, not ethnicity
  - many are inherited or based on genetics

Prejudice:
- a rigid and irrational generalization or attitude about an entire category of people
- may or may not result in discrimination
  - prejudice is an attitude, while discrimination is an action

Race Categorization:
- categorization of people in racial terms
- lacks biological basis
- it is society, not biology, which creates racial categories
- often used as a means of social stratification, based on physical differences society deems to be socially significant

Social Solidarity:
- ability of a social group to maintain itself despite obstacles

Stereotype:

- prejudicial views or descriptions of some categories of people
- an overgeneralization about the appearance or behavior of a social group
- usually but not always perceived as offensive by the person they are directed toward

Stigma:

- a powerfully negative social label that radically changes a person's self-concept and social identity
- a mark of social disgrace where the person's deviance is recognized by others
  - many people engage secretly in deviant acts
  - as long as such individuals are not stigmatized or marked as deviant, they consider themselves to be normal

Subculture:

- values and related behaviors of a group that distinguish its members from the larger culture; a world within a world
  - e.g. the Amish, who maintain their own subculture within the larger American culture

Subordinate Groups:

- groups that are dominated by the majority groups

WASP:

- acronym for White Anglo-Saxon Protestant, often disparagingly to refer to prejudice and discrimination

Religion in Society

Altruism:
- the principle or practice of concern for the welfare of others
- the opposite of selfishness

Church:
- large and established religious body with a formal, bureaucratic structure
- features formally established leadership and an institutionalized way of dealing with money
- many members are members because their parents were, not because they voluntarily joined
- one of three main forms of religious organization (cult, sect, and church)
  - sects and cults are less organized and more informal

Cult:
- the simplest form of religious organization
- normally centers around a charismatic leader
- cult members usually reject the norms and values of the larger society

Monotheism:
- system of worship that pays respect to only one god
  - e.g. Judaism, Christianity, Islam

Polytheism:
- religion that emphasizes many gods
  - e.g. Shintoism, Hinduism, Buddhism and Taoism
- tend to focus on nature, the path to happiness, and the meaning of life

Rituals:
- oft-repeated symbolic ceremonies practices acted out by religious groups to express their beliefs
  - religious rites are often intended to evoke awe for the sacred

Sacred:
- Durkheim's term for things set apart or forbidden that inspire fear, awe, reverence, or deep respect
- may refer to religious symbols, objects, and/or rituals
- contrasts with the profane, which is nonreligious in subject matter, form, or use

Sect:
- nonconformist group typically formed in protest to an established church
- typically regarded as heretical by the larger group to which they belong or from which they eventually break off
- characterized by little formal structure and few or no leaders
- differs from a cult in that it doesn't depend on a charismatic leader for continuity

Research Methods and Terminology

Bilateral Kinship Tracing:
- where ancestry is traced through both sides of the family
- in the most common form of kinship tracing, children generally take the father's name

Control and Experimental Groups:
- In scientific research, subjects of a study are divided into two groups:
  - a control group, which is kept under normal conditions
  - an experimental group, which is subject to a particular condition of the experiment
- the researcher's goal is to observe the effect of the condition on the experimental group, and compare that effect to the control group (which hasn't experienced the condition)

Deductive Reasoning (Deductive Theory):
- reasoning from one or more general statements regarding known facts to reach a logical conclusion
  - e.g. all humans have ears, Alexander the Great was a human, therefore, Alexander the Great must have had ears
- contrasts with inductive reasoning, which constructs or evaluates general propositions that are derived from specific examples

Dependent Variables:
- the affected or manipulated variable in human development research
  - the effect is gained by altering the independent variable(s)
  - e.g. eating 10 pieces of cake (an independent variable) may make a person sick (dependent variable)
- synonymous with "effect" in sociology-related research
  - the variable that is the cause is the independent variable

Ethical Concerns in Sociological Research:
- Includes questions such as:
  - could the results of this research be used in harmful ways?
  - is the privacy of the research subjects being protected, or invaded?
  - should research subjects be notified that they are being studied?

Hawthorne Effect:
- where subjects of a research study change their behavior if they know they are being studied
- named after a study that took place at the Hawthorne Plant of Western Electric Company
  - workers improved their performance in the presence of researchers

Independent Variable:
- variable that produces an effect on another variable
  - the variable that is affected is the dependent variable
- synonymous with "cause" in sociology-related research

Inductive Reasoning:
- reasoning that evaluates general propositions derived from specific examples
  - a small observation is used to infer a larger theory, without necessarily proving it
  - many ancient philosophers used induction for making observations and constructing theories
- contrasts with deductive reasoning, in which specific examples are derived from general propositions
- also known as induction or inductive theory

Interaction Process Analysis:
- theory by Robert Bales proposing that a group alternately focuses on task oriented aspects and on relational oriented aspects during a group discussion
  - task oriented interventions are opposing one another

- - relational oriented interventions are about reinforcing one another
  - each group strives for a balance or equilibrium between these two ends of the continuum
- classifies messages into four categories: social-emotional positive, social-emotional negative, questions, and attempted answers
- used to measure leadership in face-to-face groups

Mean:
- the average of a set of numbers

Median:
- the middle value in a set of numbers

Mode:
- the number that is repeated more than any other number in a set of numbers

Participant Observation:
- research in which the researcher participates in a research setting while observing what is happening in that setting

Qualitative Methods of Research:
- where emphasis is placed on observing, describing, and drawing conclusions from people's behavior
  - not exact science like quantitative methods, which are based on statistics and math

Quantitative Methods of Research:
- research in which emphasis is placed on precise measurement, numbers, and statistics
- primarily used in the natural sciences, but also by some sociologists
- designed to achieve precision
- contrast with qualitative methods, which rely on personal observation and description to form conclusions

Representative Sample:
- a portion of the subject population which represents the whole
- involves randomly choosing subjects in such a way that each one has an equal chance of being selected
- method used when the number of subjects is too large for individual research

Secondary Analysis:
- research method in which a researcher utilizes data collected by others
- instead of going out and collecting new data, old records and documents are studied in an attempt to discover something new

Stratified Sampling:
- method of sampling specific subgroups of the target population
    - everyone in the subgroups has an equal chance of being included in the study
- relies on differences in the subject population as the basis for selecting, instead of doing a straight random selection

Survey Method:
- research method in which participants respond to a series of statements or questions
- the most commonly used research method among sociologists
- two types of survey instruments
    - interviews
    - questionnaires

Triangulation:
- a powerful technique used in sociological research
- facilitates validation of data through cross verification (double-checking results) from more than two sources

Unobtrusive Observation:
- where the subjects of research are unaware that they are being observed

Social Order and Cultural Norms

Anomie:
- the confusion that arises when social norms conflict or don't even exist
- refers to a condition of relative normlessness
    - social regulations break down
    - the controlling influence of society on individuals loses effectiveness
    - individuals are left to their own devices
- first proposed by Émile Durkheim—who stated that rapid social change led to a condition of normlessness
    - Durkheim coined the phrase anomie
- later expanded upon by Robert Merton
    - Merton proposed that there is often a gap between socially accepted goals and the means to accomplish them
        - e.g. many wish to gain wealth but do not have the means to obtain it
            - as a result they turn to deviance

Anticipatory Socialization:
- when children draw on their parents' experiences to learn about their possible future
    - children play games where they practice being students, parents, or various types of workers before they grow up
- occurs in advance of playing an actual role

Conflict Perspective or Theory:
- views society as characterized by conflict and inequality
    - social groups are engaged in a continual competition for access to and control of scarce resources
    - some groups remain privileged, while others struggle to survive
        - the elite control the poor
    - social order something imposed on the weak and poor by the rich and powerful

- focuses on the negative and conflicted nature of society, looking for conflict rather than function in any situation
  - those who own the means of production are pitted against those who do not
  - those who get all the benefits are struggling with those who do not
- proposes that inequality is an inherent result of differences in power among social groups
- assumes that social institutions reflect male dominance
- encourages social change

Cultural Capital:
- social assets such as values, beliefs, attitudes, and competencies in language and culture
  - students with the most cultural capital are more highly rewarded by the educational system

Cultural Pluralism:
- when different societal groups maintain parts of their distinctive cultures while coexisting peacefully with the majority group
  - newcomers conform outwardly to values and norms as a way to adapt
    - e.g. immigrants might learn a new language, use the national currency, or obey cultural norms viewed as necessary for success, while holding on to the music and religion of their prior culture

Cultural Relativism:
- efforts of sociologists to be objective and avoid allowing ethnocentrism to affect their study of other cultures
- sociologists should focus only on the reason an observed element exists and avoid imposing their own meaning on what is observed

Culture:
- the beliefs, behaviors, objects, and other characteristics common to the members of a particular group or society
- consists of two types:

- Material Culture: physical objects, resources, and spaces that people use to define their culture
- Non-material Culture: the nonphysical ideas that people have about their culture, including beliefs, values, rules, norms, morals, language, organizations, and institutions

Functionalist Theory or Perspective:
- theoretical framework that sees society as a complex system whose parts work together to promote solidarity and stability
- within the field of sociology, functionalist theory proposes that each social institution serves functions that contribute to the needs of the society as a whole
  - e.g. the role of mothers as nurturers and caregivers insures that important societal tasks will be fulfilled and family members needs will be provided for

Gemeinschaft:
- one of two types of social groups as defined by Ferdinand Tonnies
- association in which individuals are oriented to the large association as much as, if not more than, to their own self-interest
- members are regulated by common mores, or beliefs about the appropriate behavior and responsibility of members of the association
- best exemplified by the family unit

Gesellschaft:
- one of two types of social groups as defined by Ferdinand Tonnies
- the group is goal-oriented and membership is based on contractual relationships
- often translated as society
  - e.g. a village or town

Human Ecology:
- study of the relationship between people and their physical environment
- first considered by University of Chicago sociologists who studied the city during the early decades of the 20th century

Interactionist Theory:
- sociological study on how meaning is created in face-to-face interactions between individuals

Latent Function:
- the unintended consequences of people's actions that help keep a social system in equilibrium

Law of Three Stages:
- an idea developed by Auguste Comte
- proposes that society as a whole, and each particular science, develops through three mentally conceived stages:
  1. the theological stage
  2. the metaphysical stage, and
  3. the positive stage

Manifest Function:
- the intended consequences of people's actions designed to help some part of a social system

Material Culture:
- material objects that distinguish a group of people, such as art, buildings, weapons, utensils, machines, hairstyles, clothing, and jewelry
- anything that is material or physically exists, which people attach meaning to and use

Mores:
- cultural or ethical norms that are strictly enforced because they are thought essential to core values
  - violation of a culture's mores results in strong criticism or even punishment

Nonmaterial Culture:
- a group's ways of thinking (including its beliefs, values, and other assumptions about the world) and doing (its common patterns of behavior, including language and other forms of interaction)

Normative Organizations:
- groups that people voluntarily join to pursue common interests

Norms:
- rules and expectations by which a society guides the behavior of its members
- often vary from culture to culture
- can be broken down into folkways, mores, taboos, and laws

Out-Group:
- social group to which an individual does not identify
- contrasts with an in-group, a social group to which a person psychologically identifies as being a member

Peer Group:
- group of people linked together by common interests, equal social position, and usually similar age
- association of self-selected equals, based on friendship, a sense of belonging, and acceptance
- competes with the family for first place as the dominant group in a person's life

Personality:
- a person's fairly consistent patterns of thinking, feeling, and acting
- developed through socialization
- humans who don't grow up socializing around other humans don't develop personalities

Primary socialization:
- socialization which begins at birth and continues until the child / person is a member of society as a social being

Reference Group:
- social group that serves as a point of reference in making evaluations or decisions
- standard by which we evaluate ourselves
- strongly influences behavior and social attitudes

Reform Movement:
- movement focused on improving society by changing some specific aspect of the social structure

Resocialization:
- deliberate socialization intended to radically alter an individual's personality
- involves discarding behavioral practices and adopting new ones
- happens for various reasons throughout life (e.g. getting married, becoming a parent, taking on a new and prestigious job, etc.)

Resource Mobilization Theory:
- theory that social movements succeed or fail based on their ability to mobilize resources such as time, money, and people's skills
- focuses on the ability of social movers and shakers to obtain resources and mobilize people to advance their cause
- resources are defined as money, time, skills, mass media access, and materials
- special emphasis is placed on the acquisition of financial resources from various sources

Sapir-Whorf Hypothesis:
- the assertion that people perceive the world only in terms of the symbols contained in their language
- proposes that languages provide mental categories that determine how speakers of that language think
- based on the hypothesis that language precedes thought

Secondary Socialization:
- follows primary socialization
- socialization which an already socialized person experiences

Social Control:

- attempts by society to regulate the thought and behavior of individuals with an end goal of encouraging conformity to social norms
  - internal social control is known as socialization
    - informal social control
    - based on approval or disapproval of people whose opinion matters to the deviant
  - external social control may be exerted through persuasion, teaching, sanctions, or force
    - a formal social control
    - involves people who are in a position to enforce norms

Social Epidemiology:

- study of the causes and distribution of health, disease, and impairment throughout a population

Social Movement:

- a large group of people organized to promote or resist social change through collective action
  - e.g. the Civil Rights Movement, Right to Life Movement, or Temperance Movement

Socialization:

- the lifelong process of social interaction through which individuals acquire a self-identity and the physical, mental, and social skills needed for survival in society
- means of learning the attitudes, values, and actions appropriate to a culture
- divided into two types:
  - primary socialization—occurs from birth until the person enters society
  - secondary socialization—second tier of socialization, occurs after primary socialization is finished

Socialization Agents:
- the driving forces behind socialization
    - individuals, groups, and institutions which facilitate socialization
    - include family, friends, peers, school, work, religion, and mass media

Society:
- term used by sociologists to refer to a group of people who share a culture and a territory

Sociocultural Evolution:
- process of change that results from a society's gaining new information, particularly technology
    - as time passes, society becomes more complex.

Sociological Imagination:
- ability to see the relationship between individual experiences and the larger society
- an understanding that social forces affect individual lives and that individuals can alter the course of human history
- a concept developed by C. Wright Mills

Sociological Perspectives:
- three theoretical points of view from which sociologists study society
    - symbolic interactionism
    - functionalism
    - conflict theory

Sociology:
- the systematic study of human society
- the study of human social behavior—societies, social groups, and the relationships between people

Sociometry:
- a quantitative method for measuring social relationships
- helps researchers to determine who is interacting with whom and find the direction of interaction in a small group
- developed by Jacob L. Moreno

Symbolic Interactionism:
- theoretical perspective in which society is viewed as composed of symbols that people use to establish meaning, develop their views of the world, and communicate with one another
- examines the role of symbols in attaching meaning to human interaction
  - symbols examined include signs, gestures, dress, and language

Taboos:
- norms so strong that violation triggers revulsion
  - so negative as to be considered unthinkable or unspeakable
  - absolutely forbidden by a culture
  - e.g. incest, cannibalism

Theory of Relative Deprivation:
- proposes that people who are satisfied with their present condition are less likely to seek change

Value-added Model:
- proposes that social movements develop in response to certain inciting incidents or dramatic events called precipitating factors

Values:
- broad preferences concerning appropriate courses of action or outcomes

Verstehen:

- synonymous with "empathetic understanding"
- allows sociologists to mentally put themselves into the "other person's shoes," thereby obtaining an "interpretative understanding" of individual behavior
- term coined by Max Weber

Social Status, Stratification, and Roles

Achieved Status:
- when an individual achieves status because of something he or she did (e.g. wife, husband, student)

Ascribed Status:
- status that is obtained through birth or some other reason beyond an individual's control (e.g. race, gender, inheritance, widowhood)

Caste System:
- system of social stratification which allows little social mobility
  - people are born or married into a certain position (e.g. India, where it is practically impossible to alter status in life)
  - the opposite of the achieved status social stratification system of the United States

Division of Labor:
- method of dividing work within a social group or organization

Dramaturgy:
- theory proposing that social interaction is like a drama or play
  - people play roles much as actors do, attempting to control the reactions of others by presenting a certain image of one's self
  - developed by Erving Goffman

Functionalist View of Social Stratification:
- emphasizes mutualistic relations between elites and commoners
  - elites are seen as providing managerial benefits
  - the commoners' part of the bargain is to produce the surplus necessary to adequately reward these services

- society must offer greater rewards and higher status for certain positions because they require more training and sacrifice
- the most qualified people end up in the most demanding positions, an inevitable result of social stratification
- developed and proposed by Kingsley Davis and Wilbert E. Moore

Halo Effect:
- when people are stereotyped based on earlier impressions
- those impressions color future events
- stereotypes may be positive or negative
  - e.g. physically attractive people may be perceived as being especially kind or intelligent

Horizontal Mobility:
- movement from one position to another within the same social level
  - e.g. switching from one dishwashing job to another
- in contrast to vertical mobility, which is movement of individuals or groups up (or down) from one socio-economic level to another

Impression Management:
- when people attempt to control the impressions they make on others by playing their social roles in a competent way
- also known as a presentation of one's self

In-Group:
- a social group to which a person psychologically identifies as being a member
- contrasts with an out-group, which is a social group to which an individual does not identify

Intergenerational Mobility:
- a change in social standing across generations
- occurs during a person's lifetime
- also known as career mobility

Master Status:
- status that has exceptional importance for social identity, often shaping a person's entire life
- the status a person is most identified with—and the most important one they hold
  - others generally assume that a person possesses certain traits associated with their master status

Nature of Self:
- "Self" is split into two parts—"Me" and "I"
  - "Me" is the social self
    - the response of an individual to the attitudes of others
    - focuses on conformity with the expectations of society
  - "I" is the response to the "Me"
    - the organized set of attitudes of others which an individual assumes
    - all human acts begin in the form of "I"
    - the creative aspect that gives energy to an act

Prestige:
- the respect or regard with which a person is looked upon by others

Role Conflict:
- incompatibility between roles when expectations attached to one role conflict with expectations of another role
  - e.g. a mother's job may conflict with her responsibilities as a parent

Role Exit:
- when people disengage from social roles that have been central to their self-identity
  - the person "exiting" often adopts new roles leading to new identities

Role Strain
- incompatibility among roles corresponding to a single status
  - e.g. managers may socialize with subordinates while simultaneously maintaining a large enough distance to function as their supervisor

Role Taking:
- assuming the perspective of another person in order to feel more empathy

Social Devaluation:
- occurs when a person or group is considered to have less social value than other persons or groups
  - often experienced by ageing adults in industrial societies, where prestige is largely based on occupational status

Social Hierarchy:
- ranks people into social statuses
- results from social stratification
  - people are born into ascribed social positions
  - achieved social positions result from personal ability or effort

Social Marginality:
- state of being part insider and part outsider within a social structure
  - often experienced by immigrants who simultaneously share the life and traditions of two distinct social groups

Social Mobility:
- movement up or down the social hierarchy ladder
- opportunities for social mobility vary between societies
  - social mobility in India, where a person is born or married into his or her social position, ranges from difficult to impossible
  - social mobility in America's class system presents fewer barriers and occurs more often

Social Stratification:
- division of large numbers of people into layers according to their relative power, property, and prestige
- applies both to nations and people within a nation, society, or other group
- involves the unequal distribution of power, property, and prestige
- believed by Karl Marx to be the result of class structure
  - exploitation of the "have nots" by those who have
  - power of the Bourgeoisie over the Proletariat

Status:
- social ranking, or the position an individual occupies in society or a social group
- linked to personal prestige, social honor, or popularity in a society

Status Set:
- all of the statuses a person holds at a given time
  - e.g. a woman could be a wife, mother, daughter, and physician all at the same time

Vertical Mobility:
- movement of individuals or groups from one socio-economic level to another
- may be either upward or downward
  - e.g. up the corporate ladder, downward into poverty
- contrasts with horizontal mobility, which is movement from one position to another within the same social level
  - e.g. switching from one dishwashing job to another

Urban Growth, Government, and Demographics

Authoritarian Government:
- dictator-like government where subjects have little or no say in civil affairs
- opposition to authority is not tolerated
- popular participation in government is denied
- one of three main types of government (the other two are totalitarian and democratic)

Authority:
- power that is viewed by the people as legitimate rather than coercive

Bureaucracy:
- a formal organization where whose goal is to perform complex tasks as efficiently as possible
- generally guided by inflexible written rules and procedures
- features a strict hierarchy of authority
- composed of highly specialized jobs
- the classic model of modern bureaucracy was proposed by German sociologist Max Weber, who believed:
  - the formation of bureaucracies was inevitable due to the complex nature of modern life and the growing demands of citizens

City:
- permanent settlement of people with a dense population
  - each city is characterized by a different group of people and activity

City-State:
- city whose power extends to adjacent areas
- centralized political powers that came into being as cities developed and grew

Community:
- a social unit that shares a common location or values and provides people with a sense of identity or feeling of belonging

Concentric Zone Growth Model:
- early theoretical models to explain urban social structures
- developed by sociologist Ernest Burgess in 1924
- views a city as a series of rings, each characterized by a different type of land use
  - consists of five zones:
    - Zone 1: central business district and cultural center, in the heart of the city
    - Zone 2: transition zoned with mixed business and residential use
    - Zone 3: working class residential homes
    - Zone 4: near the edge of the city, better quality middle class homes
    - Zone 5: commuters
- more complex than the traditional down-mid-uptown divide where:
  - downtown is the central business district
  - uptown is the affluent residential outer ring
  - midtown in everything between

Concentric Zone Growth Theory:
- the theory behind the Concentric Zone Growth Model
- developed by Ernest Burgess
- model of city growth where cities grow in a series of rings or concentric circles
- the rings or circles are based on the amount that people are willing to pay for the land
- the value of land are based on the profits obtainable from owning that land (known as the "Bid Rent Curve")
  - the center of town may have the highest number of customers, making it most profitable for retail stores
  - manufacturers will pay slightly less for the land, as they are only interested in accessibility for workers and goods "in and out"
  - residential land takes up the surrounding land

Democracy (Democratic Government):
- system of government where the people hold power either directly or through elected representatives
- citizens meet regularly to debate and make decisions on current issues
- the people are granted the right to participate in government, and ultimately hold the authority over how they are governed
- contrasts with authoritarian or totalitarian governments, where the rulers make all decisions and tolerate no opposition

Demographic Transition Theory:
- proposes that birth and death rates decrease as a society becomes more technologically advanced and industrialized

Demography:
- the study of populations and their characteristics and changes
- categorizes people into groups by factors such as age, gender, education, occupation, income, or family background

Density:
- measurement of the population living in a specific geographic are
  - e.g. number of people per square mile

Formal Organization:
- a secondary group with a goal-directed agenda
- characterized by formality, ranked positions, and complex division of labor
- includes informal relations among workers, which usually improve worker satisfaction and productivity

Gentrification:
- when members of the middle and upper class move into a central city area and renovate existing properties
  - controversial because it often displaces poor people who can no longer afford to live in affected neighborhoods

Immigration:
- the act of people entering and settling in a country or region to which they are not native

Invasion-Succession Cycle:
- the process of one group of people displacing a group whose racial-ethnic or social class characteristics differ from their own
  - e.g. low-income neighborhood residents spill over into adjacent middle-class neighborhoods and the middle class to move out

Megalopolis:
- urban area consisting of at least two metropolises and their many suburbs
- created when the suburbs surrounding several metropolises grow and merge together, forming one continuous urban complex

Metropolis:
- large city or urban area that socially and economically dominates the surrounding area
- serves as a significant economic, political and cultural center
  - New York City is considered to be the first metropolis

Over-urbanization:
- where population growth outpaces industrial growth, beyond the capacity of the existing structure to cope with them

Parkinson's Law:
- states that in a bureaucratic organization, "work expands to fill the time available for its completion"
  - bureaucracies grow because managers continue to hire people to look busy and expand their "empire"
  - instead of focusing on what needs to be done, managers create more work to fill the available time

Population Natural Growth Rate:
- calculated by subtracting the death rate from the birth rate and dividing by 10

Poverty levels:

- poverty occurs primarily due to low worker wages
- Caucasians (whites) make up the largest ethnic group in poverty
- the poverty rate (percentage of an ethnic group in poverty) is highest among African Americans and Native Americans
  - 25% of African and Native Americans live in poverty
  - 11% of Caucasians (whites) live in poverty
- 20% of children living in the United States are poverty-stricken
  - sociologist believe the high rate of child poverty is due to the sharp increase in out-of-wedlock births
    - unmarried women account for 1 in 3 United States births today
    - this is in contrast to 1 in 20 in 1960
- the rate of children in poverty has always been higher than that of the total population
  - children are at a much greater risk of poverty than older people
- poverty among the elderly in the United States has fallen since the 1970's
- prior to the mid-1970s, persons aged 65 and older were much more likely to be poor than other Americans
  - poverty level among the elderly has been less than the national poverty level since 1982

Problems of City Life:

- large numbers of people living in a relatively small amount of space (crowding)
- a wide variety of income levels
- the need to fairly provide city services for residents of all classes and income levels

Push Factors:

- encourage people to leave one area and move to another
  - e.g. political unrest, violence, inadequate school systems, and famine

Rational Legal Authority:
- authority based on rational grounds
  - usually a body of laws or rules which have been legally enacted or contractually established

Rural Sociology:
- subfield of sociology that examines social relationships and political and economic structures in less populated areas

Sector Model:
- proposes that cities grow outwards in sectors according to the location of physical features such as rivers and transportation lines

State:
- formal organization with the legal and political authority to regulate relationships among society members inside and outside of the society
- also referred to as the government

Suburban Neighborhood:
- urban area beyond the political boundaries of a city
- tend to be organized by class, income level, or race

Totalitarian Government:
- where rulers exercise absolute and centralized control over all aspects of life
- even more regulated than an authoritarian government
  - takes government one step further by reaching into all realms of life

Typology of Urban Dwellers:
- identified by sociologist Herbert Gans
- useful in understanding life in urban areas
- comprised of five types of city residents:
  - cosmopolites
    - students, writers, musicians, and intellectuals who live in a city because of its cultural attractions and other amenities

- unmarried and childless individuals
  - live in a city to be near their jobs and enjoy the various kinds of entertainment found in a metropolitan area
- ethnic villagers
  - recent immigrants and members of various ethnic groups
  - who live an ethnic neighborhood with a strong sense of community and powerful social bonds
- the deprived
  - uneducated, poverty-stricken people who are unemployed, underemployed, or underpaid
  - live in neighborhoods filled with trash, broken windows, and other signs of disorder
  - commit high rates of crime and also have high rates of victimization by crime
- the trapped
  - residents who wish to leave their neighborhoods but are unable to do so for a variety of reasons, such as:
    - they are alcoholics or drug addicts
    - they are elderly and disabled
    - they are jobless and cannot afford to move to a better area

Urban Sociology:
- subfield of sociology that examines social relationships and political and economic structures in metropolitan areas

Urbanization Theories:
- attempt to determine patterns in the development or urban growth in metropolitan areas
  - e.g. the Multiple Nuclei Theory, Concentric Zone theory, and the Sector theory

Urbanization:
- process by which an increasing proportion of a population lives in cities rather than rural areas